OTHER HELEN EXLEY GIFTBOOKS:

Thoughts on Being at Peace
Thoughts on Being Happy
The Precious Present
Seize the day! Enjoy the moment!
Words of Wisdom
Words on Solitude and Silence
Words on Joy
Words on a Simple Life

Published simultaneously in 1999 by Exley Publications Ltd in Great Britain,
and Exley Publications LLC in the USA.

4   6   8   10   12   11   9   7   5

Selection and arrangement copyright © Helen Exley 1999.
The moral right of the author has been asserted.

ISBN 1-86187-114-7

Words and pictures selected by Helen Exley.
Pictures researched by Image Select International.
Printed in China.

Exley Publications Ltd, 16 Chalk Hill, Watford, Herts WD1 4BN, UK.
Exley Publications LLC, 232 Madison Avenue, Suite 1206, NY 10016, USA.

WISDOM OF THE MILLENNIUM

A HELEN EXLEY GIFTBOOK

NEW YORK • WATFORD, UK

KINDNESS

IS MORE IMPORTANT

THAN WISDOM,

AND THE RECOGNITION

OF THIS

IS THE BEGINNING

OF WISDOM.

THEODORE ISAAC RUBIN

To love is to risk not being loved in return.
To hope is to risk disappointment.
But risks must be taken because the greatest risk in life
is to risk nothing.
The person who risks nothing, does nothing,
sees nothing, has nothing and is nothing.
He cannot learn, feel, change, grow, love and live.

AUTHOR UNKNOWN

LIFE IS SHORT

AND WE HAVE NOT

TOO MUCH TIME FOR

GLADDENING THE HEARTS

OF THOSE WHO

ARE TRAVELLING THE DARK

WAY WITH US.

OH, BE SWIFT TO LOVE!

MAKE HASTE TO BE KIND.

HENRI FREDERIC AMIEL
(1821-1881)

I expect to pass through life but once. If therefore, there be any kindness I can show, or any good thing I can do to any fellow being, let me do it now, and not defer or neglect it, as I shall not pass this way again.

WILLIAM PENN (1644 - 1718)

The world has no room for cowards.
We must all be ready somehow to toil,
to suffer, to die. And yours is not the less noble
because no drum beats before you
when you go out into your daily battlefields,
and no crowds shout about your coming
when you return from your daily victory
or defeat.

ROBERT LOUIS STEVENSON (1850-1894)

Success seems to be largely

a matter of hanging on after others have let go.

WILLIAM FEATHER

Stand through life firm as a rock in the sea,

undisturbed and unmoved by its ever-rising waves.

HAZRAT INAYAT KHAN (1882-1927)

*Wisdom means keeping a sense
of the fallibility of all our views
and opinions, and of the uncertainty
and instability of the things
we most count on.*

GERARD BROWN

ONLY IN GROWTH, REFORM AND CHANGE,

PARADOXICALLY ENOUGH,

IS TRUE SECURITY TO BE FOUND.

ANNE MORROW LINDBERGH, b. 1906

Love alone

is capable of uniting

living beings

in such a way

as to complete

and fulfil them,

for it alone

takes them

and joins them

by what is deepest

in themselves.

PIERRE TEILHARD DE CHARDIN
(1881-1955)

HE ALONE IS GREAT

WHO TURNS THE VOICE OF THE WIND

INTO A SONG MADE SWEETER

BY HIS OWN LOVING.

KAHLIL GIBRAN
(1883-1931)

You can have
anything you want if you want it
desperately enough.
You must want it
with an exuberance that erupts
through the skin and joins the energy
that created the world.

SHEILA GRAHAM

There is no such thing as a great talent without great will-power.

HONORE DE BALZAC (1799-1850)

I was taught
that the way of progress
is neither swift nor easy.

MARIE CURIE (1867-1934)

I LONG TO ACCOMPLISH A GREAT AND NOBLE TASK,
BUT IT IS MY CHIEF DUTY TO ACCOMPLISH SMALL TASKS
AS IF THEY WERE GREAT AND NOBLE.

HELEN KELLER

(1 8 8 0 - 1 9 6 8)

Take time to be friendly — It is the road to happiness.

Take time to dream — It is hitching your wagon to a star.

Take time to love and to be loved — It is the privilege of the gods.

Take time to look around — It is too short a day to be selfish.

Take time to laugh — It is the music of the soul.

OLD ENGLISH

Learn from the past.
Do not come to the end of your life
only to find you have not lived.
For many come to the point of leaving the
space of the earth
and when they gaze back,
they see the joy and the beauty
that could not be theirs because
of the fears they lived.

CLEARWATER

DON'T HURRY,
DON'T WORRY.
YOU'RE ONLY HERE
FOR A SHORT VISIT.
SO BE SURE TO STOP AND
SMELL THE FLOWERS.

WALTER HAGEN

Life is not easy for any of us.
But what of that? We must
have perseverance and above all
confidence in ourselves.
We must believe that we are
gifted for something, and that
this thing, at whatever cost,
must be attained.

MARIE CURIE (1867-1934)

"ZIDELE AMATHAMBO."
GIVE YOURSELF UP,
BONES AS WELL.
(i.e. take a chance!)

SOUTH AFRICAN
NDEBELE SAYING

How can you hesitate? Risk!
Risk anything!
Care no more for the opinion
of others, for those voices.
Do the hardest thing on earth
for you. Act for yourself.
Face the truth.

KATHERINE MANSFIELD
(1888-1923)

If you want others to be happy,
practice compassion.
If you want to be happy,
practice compassion.

DALAI LAMA, b.1935

When you carry out
acts of kindness
you get
a wonderful feeling
inside.
It is as though
something inside your body
responds
and says, Yes,
this is how
I ought to feel.

RABBI HAROLD KUSHNER

... something inside your body responds

BE KIND –
EVERYONE YOU MEET
IS FIGHTING A HARD BATTLE.

JOHN WATSON

It made me feel

When I was going through a very difficult time,
someone called me up and played piano music for me
on my answering machine. It made me feel very loved,
and I never discovered who did it.

THE EDITORS OF CONARI PRESS,
FROM "RANDOM ACTS OF KINDNESS"

very loved

THROW OUT THE LIFELINE,
THROW OUT THE LIFELINE,
SOMEONE IS SINKING TODAY.

EDWARD SMITH UFFORD

You can transcend all negativity
when you realize that the only power
it has over you is your belief in it.
As you experience this truth
about yourself you are set free.

EILEEN CADDY

I was always looking outside myself
for strength and confidence
but it comes from within.
It is there all the time.

ANNA FREUD

*... if you want something
very badly, you can achieve it.
It may take patience,
very hard work,
a real struggle, and a long time;
but it can be done.
That much faith
is a prerequisite
of any undertaking,
artistic or otherwise.*

MARGO JONES (1913-1955)

We ought to remember
that we are not the only ones
to find ourselves
at an apparent impasse.
Just as a kite rises
against the wind,
even the worst of troubles
can strengthen us.
As thousands before us
have met the identical fate
and mastered it, so can we!

DR. R. BRASCH

You are of a species bred to endure. The sufferings of others do not make your own less real - but remember how those others clung to life and, in the end, won through. You can do it.

PAM BROWN, b.1928

You gain strength,
courage, and confidence
by every experience in which
you really stop
to look fear in the face.
You are able to say to yourself,
"I lived through this horror.
I can take the next thing
that comes along."
... You must do the thing you
think you cannot do.

I lived through this...

Courage is, with love,
the greatest gift.
We are, each of us, defeated
many times – but if we accept
defeat with cheerfulness,
and learn from it,
and try another way –
then we will find
fulfilment.

ROSANNE AMBROSE-BROWN

THE GLORY
IS NOT IN NEVER FAILING,
BUT IN RISING EVERY TIME
YOU FALL.

CHINESE PROVERB

W hat do we live for,
if it is not to make life less difficult for each other?

GEORGE ELIOT (MARY ANN EVANS) (1819-1880)

Happiness is a perfume

you cannot pour on others

without getting a few drops on yourself.

RALPH WALDO EMERSON
(1803-1882)

It is in the shelter of each other
that the people live.

IRISH PROVERB

THE CURE FOR ALL
THE ILLS AND WRONGS,
THE CARES, THE SORROWS
AND CRIMES OF HUMANITY,
ALL LIE IN
THAT ONE WORD "LOVE".
IT IS THE DIVINE VITALITY
THAT PRODUCES
AND RESTORES LIFE.
TO EACH AND EVERY ONE
OF US IT GIVES THE POWER
OF WORKING MIRACLES,
IF WE WILL.

LYDIA M. CHILD
(1802-1880)

I am done with great things and big plans, great institutions and big success. I am for those tiny, invisible loving human forces that work from individual to individual, creeping through the crannies of the world like so many rootlets, or like the capillary oozing of water, which, if given time, will rend the hardest monuments of pride.

From success you get lots of things,
but not that great inside thing
that love brings you.

SAM GOLDWYN (1882-1974)

WHEN
A BLIND MAN
CARRIES
A LAME MAN,
BOTH
GO FORWARD.

SWEDISH PROVERB

It is one of the most
beautiful compensations
of life that no man can
sincerely try to help another
without
helping himself.

RALPH WALDO EMERSON
(1803-1882)

One of the most difficult
things to give away
is kindness,
for it is usually returned.

MARK ORTMAN

There are no impossible dreams,
just our limited perception
of what is possible.

BETH MENDE CONNY

You are everything that is, your
thoughts, your life, your dreams
come true. You are everything you
choose to be. You are as unlimited as
the endless universe.

SHAD HELMSTETTER

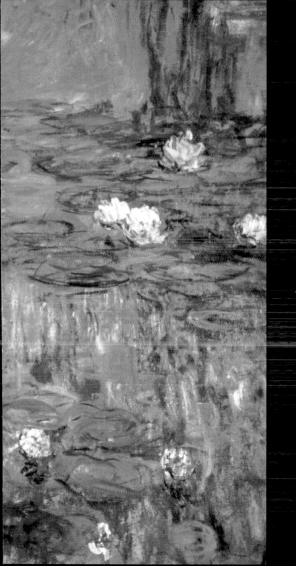

EACH SECOND
YOU CAN BE REBORN
EACH SECOND
THERE CAN BE
A NEW BEGINNING.
IT IS CHOICE.
IT IS YOUR CHOICE.

CLEARWATER

To become a champion,
fight one more round

JAMES J. CORBETT (1866-1933)

YOU NEVER REALLY LOSE
UNTIL YOU QUIT TRYING.

MIKE DITKA

Whether you think you can
or you can't, you're right!

HENRY FORD (1863-1947)

Empathy
is your pain
in my heart.

AUTHOR UNKNOWN

Then and there I invented this rule for myself to be applied to every decision I might have to make in the future. I would sort out all the arguments and see which belonged to fear and which to creativeness, and other things being equal I would make the decision which had the larger number of creative reasons on its side. I think it must be a rule something like this that makes jonquils and crocuses come pushing through the cold mud.

KATHARINE BUTLER HATHAWAY

We can cure physical diseases
with medicine
but the only cure for loneliness,
despair and hopelessness is love.
There are many in the world
who are dying
for a piece of bread
but there are many more dying
for a little love.

MOTHER TERESA

(1910-1997)

WHERE THERE IS GREAT LOVE THERE ARE ALWAYS MIRACLES.

WILLA CATHER (1876-1947)

*I compared notes
with one of my friends
who expects everything
of the universe,
and is disappointed
when anything
is less than the best,
and I found that I begin
at the other extreme,
expecting nothing,
and am always
full of thanks
for moderate goods.*

RALPH WALDO EMERSON
(1803-1882)

When indeed shall we learn that we are all related one to the other, that we are all members of one body? Until the spirit of love for our fellow men, regardless of race, color or creed, shall fill the world, making real in our lives and our deeds the actuality of human brotherhood – until the great mass of the people shall be filled with the sense of responsibility for each other's welfare, social justice can never be attained.

HELEN KELLER (1880 1968)

Life only demands
from the strength
you possess.
Only one feat
is possible — not to
have to run away.

DAG HAMMARSKJOLD (1905-1961)

The best way out is always through.

ROBERT FROST (1874-1963)

Give us grace,
O God, to dare to do the deed
which we well know cries to be done.
Let us not hesitate because of ease,
or the words of [people's] mouths,
or our own lives.
Mighty causes are calling us —
the freeing of women, the training
of children, the putting down of hate
and murder and poverty —
all these and more.
But they call with voices that mean work
and sacrifice and death.
[May we find a way to meet the task.]

W. E. B. DU BOIS (1868-1963)

W<small>E</small> HAVE ENOUGH PEOPLE
WHO TELL IT LIKE IT IS —
NOW WE COULD USE A FEW
WHO TELL IT LIKE IT CAN BE.

ROBERT ORBEN

... VICTORY IS OFTEN A THING DEFERRED, AND RARELY AT THE SUMMIT OF COURAGE.... WHAT IS AT THE SUMMIT OF COURAGE, I THINK, IS FREEDOM. THE FREEDOM THAT COMES WITH THE KNOWLEDGE THAT NO EARTHLY POWER CAN BREAK YOU; THAT AN UNBROKEN SPIRIT IS THE ONLY THING YOU CANNOT LIVE WITHOUT; THAT IN THE END IT IS THE COURAGE OF CONVICTION THAT MOVES THINGS, THAT MAKES ALL CHANGE POSSIBLE.

PAULA GIDDINGS

All serious daring

Shrug off the restraints
that you have allowed others
to place upon you.
You are limitless.
There is nothing you
cannot achieve.
There is no sadness in life
That cannot be reversed....

CLEARWATER

starts from within.

EUDORA WELTY, b.1909

To compose our character
is our duty....
Our great and glorious masterpiece
is to live appropriately.
All other things,
to rule,
to lay up treasure,
to build,
are at most but little
appendices and props....

MICHEL DE MONTAIGNE
(1533-1592)

respons

I don't think of myself
as a poor deprived
ghetto girl who made good.
I think of myself
as somebody
who from an early age
knew I was responsible
for myself,
and I had to make good.

OPRAH WINFREY, b. 1954

It had been repeated experience
that when you said to life
calmly and firmly (but very firmly!).
" I trust you; do what you must,"
life had an uncanny way of
responding to your need.

OLGA ILYIN

The old happiness is withered and dead.
But, see, there is greenness veiling the land...
the frail beginnings of a new and better life.

PAM BROWN, b. 1928

Our way is not soft grass,
it's a mountain path
with lots of rocks.
But it goes upwards, forward,
toward the sun.

RUTH WESTHEIMER, b.1928

Hold on; hold fast; hold out. Patience is genius.

COMTE DÉ BUFFON

Storms make oaks
take deeper root.

GEORGE HERBERT
(1593-1633)

The most I can do for my friend
is simply to be his friend.
I have no wealth to bestow on him.
If he knows that I am happy in loving him,
he will want no other reward.

HENRY DAVID THOREAU (1817-1862)

give friendship

Often with the poorest people
you cannot completely
alleviate their problem
but by being with them,
whatever you can do for them
makes a difference.

BROTHER GEOFF,
THE MISSIONARIES OF CHARITY BROTHERS

Without
the human community
one single human
being cannot survive.

THE DALAI LAMA, b.1935

So long as little children
are allowed to suffer,
there is no true love in this world.

ISADORA DUNCAN (1878-1927)

I had found a kind of serenity, a new maturity....
I didn't feel better or stronger than anyone else
but it seemed no longer important
whether everyone loved me or not —
more important now was for me to love them.
Feeling that way turns your whole life around;
living becomes the act of giving.

BEVERLY SILLS, b.1929

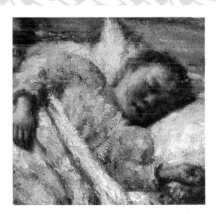

I want to beg you, as much as I can,
to be patient toward all that is unsolved
in your heart and to try to love the questions
themselves like locked rooms and like books
that are written in a very foreign tongue.
Do not seek the answers, which cannot
be given you because you would not be able
to live them.
And the point is to live everything.
Live the questions now.
Perhaps you will then gradually,
without noticing it, live along
some distant day into the answer.

RAINER MARIA RILKE
(1875-1926)

If our people
are to fight their way up
out of bondage
we must arm them with the sword
and the shield
and the buckler of pride —
belief in themselves
and their possibilities,
based upon a sure knowledge
of the achievements of the past.

MARY MCLEOD BETHUNE (1975-1955)

THE MAN
WITH COURAGE
IS A MAJORITY.

ANDREW JACKSON (1767-1845)

I have accepted fear as a part of life –
specifically the fear of change....
I have gone ahead despite the pounding
in the heart that says: turn back.

ERICA JONG, b.1942.

KEEP
HOPE
ALIVE

HOLD YOUR HEAD HIGH,
STICK YOUR CHEST OUT.
YOU CAN MAKE IT.
IT GETS DARK SOMETIMES BUT MORNING COMES....
KEEP HOPE ALIVE.

JESSE JACKSON, b.1941

Happiness is if you give it away.

CHRISTOPHER HOARE, AGE 11

She gives most who gives with joy.

MOTHER TERESA (1910-1997)

IF WE DON'T
HELP EACH OTHER,
WHO WILL?

BARBARA MANDRELL, b.1948

THE CENTER
OF HUMAN NATURE
IS ROOTED
IN TEN THOUSAND
ORDINARY
ACTS OF KINDNESS
THAT DEFINE
OUR DAYS.

STEPHEN JAY GOULD

THE FIRST SPARROW OF SPRING!
THE YEAR BEGINNING WITH YOUNGER HOPE THAN EVER!

HENRY DAVID THOREAU
(1817-1862)

Walk on a rainbow trail;
walk on a trail of song,
and all about you will be beauty.
There is a way out of every dark mist,
over a rainbow trail.

NAVAJO SONG

dreams

There were many ways of breaking a heart.
Stories were full of hearts broken by love,
but what really broke a heart was taking away
its dream — whatever that dream might be.

PEARL BUCK (1892-1973)

What will see me through
the next 20 years
(and I am less sure of those 20 than I was of "forever")
is my knowledge that even in the face
of the sweeping away of all that I assumed
to be permanent, even when the universe
made it quite clear to me that I was mistaken
in my certainties, in my definitions,
I did not break.
The shattering of my sureties
did not shatter me. Stability comes from inside,
not outside....

LUCILLE CLIFTON, b. 1936

from inside

STABI

LITY

What is the best gift you ever received?

Better still, what is the best gift you ever gave?

Perhaps you will recall that in each instance,

the best gift was one that was tied

with the heartstrings of the giver,

of yourself

one that included a part of self.

WANDA FULTON

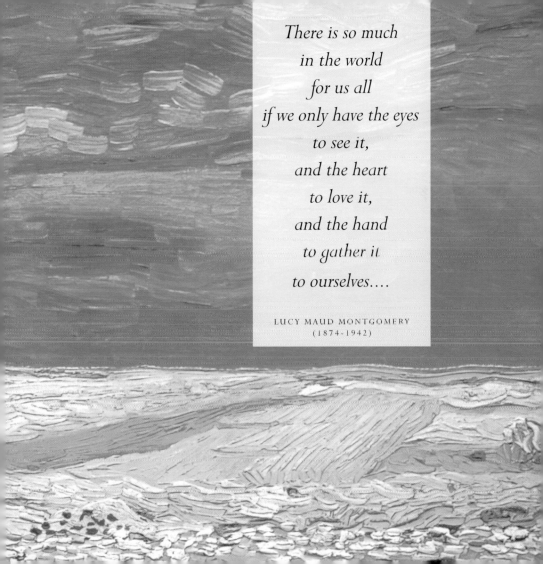

There is so much
in the world
for us all
if we only have the eyes
to see it,
and the heart
to love it,
and the hand
to gather it
to ourselves....

LUCY MAUD MONTGOMERY
(1874-1942)

Hope is the thing
with feathers
That perches in the soul
And sings the tune
without the words,
And never stops at all....

EMILY DICKINSON

(1830-1886)

Whatever life's challenges

you may face, remember always

to look to the mountaintop,

for in so doing you look to greatness.

Remember this, and let no problem,

no matter how great it may seem,

discourage you, nor let anything

less than the mountaintop

distract you. This is the one thought

I want to leave you with.

ALFONSO ORTIZ, b.1939

look to the moutain top

You shall be free indeed
when your days are not without
a care nor your nights without
a want and a grief.
But rather when these things
girdle your life and yet
you rise above them naked
and unbound.

KAHLIL GIBRAN (1883-1931)

A new life begins for us with
every second.
Let us go forward joyously to meet it.
We must press on, whether we
will or no,
and we shall walk better with
our eyes before us
than with them ever cast behind.

JEROME K. JEROME
(1859-1927)

IT ISN'T

FOR THE MOMENT

YOU ARE STRUCK

THAT YOU NEED

COURAGE,

BUT FOR THE LONG

UPHILL CLIMB

BACK TO SANITY

AND FAITH

AND SECURITY.

ANNE MORROW LINDBERGH,
b.1906

When you have gone so far

that you can't manage

one more step, then you've gone

just half the distance that you're

capable of.

GREENLAND PROVERB

Behold, we live through all things,

– famine, thirst, bereavement, pain;

all grief and misery, all woe and sorrow;

life inflicts its worst on soul and body,

– but we cannot die, though we be sick, and tired,

and faint, and worn,

lo, all things can be borne!

ELIZABETH AKERS ALLEN (1832-1911)

Without belittling the courage with which men have died,

we should not forget those acts of courage with which men...

have lived. The courage of life is often a less dramatic

spectacle than the courage of a final moment; but it is

no less a magnificent mixture of triumph and tragedy.

A man does what he must — in spite of personal

consequences, in spite of obstacles and dangers and

pressures — and that is the basis of all human morality....

JOHN F. KENNEDY (1917-1963)

"THIS TOO WILL PASS."
I WAS TAUGHT THESE WORDS BY MY GRANDMOTHER
AS A PHRASE THAT IS TO BE USED AT <u>ALL</u> TIMES
IN YOUR LIFE. WHEN THINGS ARE SPECTACULARLY
DREADFUL; WHEN THINGS ARE ABSOLUTELY APPALLING;
WHEN EVERYTHING IS SUPERB AND WONDERFUL
AND MARVELLOUS AND HAPPY —
SAY THESE FOUR WORDS TO YOURSELF.
THEY WILL GIVE YOU A SENSE OF PERSPECTIVE
AND HELP YOU ALSO TO MAKE THE MOST
OF WHAT IS GOOD AND BE STOICAL
ABOUT WHAT IS BAD.

CLAIRE RAYNER

I do the very best I know how – the very best I can; and I mean to keep doing so until the end. If the end brings me out all right, what is said against me won't amount to anything. If the end brings me out wrong, ten angels swearing I was right would make no difference.

ABRAHAM LINCOLN (1809-1865)

DO WHAT YOU CAN, WITH WHAT YOU HAVE, WHERE YOU ARE.

THEODORE ROOSEVELT (1858-1919)

I HAVE A LOT OF THINGS
TO PROVE TO MYSELF.
ONE IS THAT I CAN LIVE
MY LIFE FEARLESSLY.

OPRAH WINFREY,
b . 1 9 5 4

I DON'T THINK OF
ALL THE MISERY
BUT OF THE BEAUTY
THAT STILL REMAINS.

ANNE FRANK
(1929-1945)

There are no shortcuts to any

OUR LIVES ARE LIKE THE COURSE OF THE SUN.
AT THE DARKEST MOMENT
THERE IS PROMISE OF DAYLIGHT.

LONDON "TIMES" EDITORIAL, DECEMBER 24, 1984

place worth going. BEVERLY SILLS, b.1929

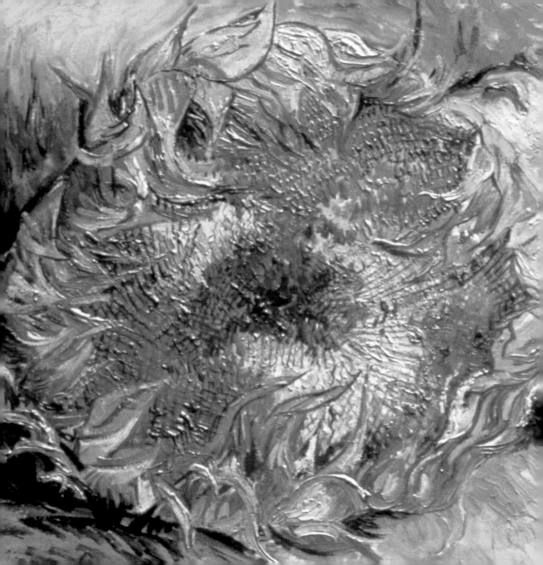

Understanding, and action proceeding from understanding and guided by it, is the one weapon against the world's bombardment, the one medicine, the one instrument by which liberty, health, and joy may be shaped or shaped toward, in the individual, and in the race.

JAMES AGEE (1909-1955), WITH WALKER EVANS

IF YOU HAVE NOT OFTEN FELT THE JOY OF DOING A KIND ACT, YOU HAVE NEGLECTED MUCH, AND MOST OF ALL YOURSELF.

A. NEILEN

Human beings who leave behind them
no great achievements, but only a sequence of small kindnesses,
have not had wasted lives.

CHARLOTTE GRAY, b. 1937

Some day,
after we have mastered
the winds, the waves,
the tides and gravity
we shall harness the energies
of love.
Then, for the second time
in the history of the world,
man will have discovered
fire.

PIERRE TEILHARD DE CHARDIN
(1881-1955)

Acknowledgements: The publishers are grateful for permission to reproduce copyright material. Whilst every effort has been made to trace copyright holders, the publishers would be pleased to hear from any not here acknowledged. KAHLIL GIBRAN: from *The Prophet* © 1923 Kahlil Gibran, renewed © 1951 Administrators C.T.A of Kahlil Gibran Estate and Mary Gibran. Published by Knopf, New York 1961. BETH MENDE CONNY used by permission of Peter Pauper Press.

LIST OF ILLUSTRATIONS
Exley Publications is very grateful to the following individuals and organizations for permission to reproduce their pictures. Whilst all reasonable efforts have been made to clear copyright and acknowledge sources and artists, Exley Publications would be happy to hear from any copyright holder who may have been omitted.

Cover, endpapers and title page: *Picos de Europa, Spain,* ZEFA.

Pages 6/7: *Blue Vase,* PAUL CÉZANNE (1839-1906), Giraudon.

Page 9: *Irises,* VINCENT VAN GOGH (1853-1890), private collection.

Page 10: *Zuiderkerk, Amsterdam,* CLAUDE MONET (1840-1926), Philadelphia Museum of Art, private collection.

Page 13: *Louveciennes: Snow,* CLAUDE MONET (1840-1926), private collection.

Page 14: *The Reader,* HENRI FANTIN-LATOUR (1836-1904), Musée d'Orsay, Paris, Art Resource.

Page 16: *Customs House at Varengeville,* CLAUDE MONET (1840-1926), Philadelphia Museum of Art, private collection.

Page 18: *Portrait of Edouard Manet at his easel,* L. HERMITTE, Giraudon.

Page 20: *Tina,* SIMON GLÜCKLICH, Archiv für Kunst.

Page 22: *A Rose Arbour and Old Well, Venice,* ELLEN FRADGLEY, Christopher Wood Gallery, London, The Bridgeman Art Library.

Pages 24/25: *The Black Sea,* IVAN CONSTANTOWITSCH AIVAZOFFSKI, Tretiakov Gallery, Moscow, The Bridgeman Art Library.

Pages 26/27: *Shades of Night,* © 1999 NESTA JENNINGS CAMPBELL, Cheltenham Art Gallery and Museums, Gloucestershire, The Bridgeman Art Library.

Pages 28/29: *Farmstead and Iris Field,* © 1999 TIMOTHY EASTON, The Bridgeman Art Library.

Page 31: *Interior, morning,* © 1999 PATRICK WILLIAM ADAM (1854-1929), Oldham Art Gallery, Lancashire, The Bridgeman Art Library.

Pages 32/33: *Sommarfrukost,* JUSTUS LUNDEGARD, Statens Konstmuseer.

Page 34: *Riverside Alley,* OSCAR STEVEN SENN, Contemporary Gallery, Jacksonville, Florida, SuperStock.

Page 37: *Young Negro Girl,* CORMON, Giraudon.

Page 39: *A Lady in an Interior,* © 1999 CARL HOLSOE, The Bridgeman Art Library.

Page 40: *Figure in the Moonlight,* JOHN ATKINSON GRIMSHAW (1836-1893), The Bridgeman Art Library.

Page 43: *Villa D'Avray,* GOROT, National Gallery of Washington, AISA.

Page 45: *Mountain Flowers,* BRUNO GUATAMACCHI, The Bridgeman Art Library.

Page 46: *Children in the Sea,* JOAQUIN SOROLLA (1863-1923), Museo Sorolla, Madrid, Index.

Pages 48/49: *Waterloo Bridge: Cloudy Weather,* CLAUDE MONET (1840-1926), Hugh Lane Municipal Gallery of Modern Art, Dublin, The Bridgeman Art Library.

Page 50: *Mother and Child,* PAUL WAGNER, The Bridgeman Art Library.

Pages 52/53: *Bay of Biscay, Brittany,* HENRY MORET (1856-1913), Hermitage Museum, St. Petersburg, SuperStock.

Pages 54/55: *Hanged Man's House,* PAUL CÉZANNE (1839-1906), Musée d'Orsay, Paris, private collection.

Pages 56/57: *Waterlillies,* CLAUDE MONET (1840-1926), Portland Art Museum, private collection.

Page 58: *Snow Scene,* DAN O'LEARY, Artworks.

Pages 60/61: *The Companions,* © 1999 ERNEST WAELVERT (1880-1946), The Bridgeman Art Library.

Page 63: *Winter Landscape with Sheep,* SIDNEY PIKE, Fine Art Photographic Library.

Pages 64/65: *Artist's Bedroom, Arles,* VINCENT VAN GOGH (1853-1890), Musée d'Orsay, Paris, private collection.